Francis Frith's
DORSET COAST

PHOTOGRAPHIC MEMORIES

Francis Frith's
DORSET COAST

◆

John Bainbridge

FRITH
BOOK Co

First published in the United Kingdom in 1999 by
Frith Book Company Ltd

Hardback Edition 1999
ISBN 1-85937-062-4

Paperback Edition 2001
ISBN 1-85937-299-6

Hardback reprinted 2001
ISBN 1-85937-062-4

British Library Cataloguing in Publication Data

Francis Frith's Dorset Coast
John Bainbridge

Frith Book Company Ltd
Frith's Barn, Teffont,
Salisbury, Wiltshire SP3 5QP
Tel: +44 (0) 1722 716 376
Email: info@frithbook.co.uk
www.frithbook.co.uk

Printed and bound in Great Britain

AS WITH ANY HISTORICAL DATABASE THE FRITH ARCHIVE IS CONSTANTLY BEING CORRECTED AND IMPROVED
AND THE PUBLISHERS WOULD WELCOME INFORMATION ON OMISSIONS OR INACCURACIES

CONTENTS

Free Mounted Print Voucher

FRANCIS FRITH: *Victorian Pioneer*

FRANCIS FRITH, Victorian founder of the world-famous photographic archive, was a complex and multitudinous man. A devout Quaker and a highly successful Victorian businessman, he was both philosophic by nature and pioneering in outlook.

By 1855 Francis Frith had already established a wholesale grocery business in Liverpool, and sold it for the astonishing sum of £200,000, which is the equivalent today of over £15,000,000. Now a multi-millionaire, he was able to indulge his passion for travel. As a child he had pored over travel books written by early explorers, and his fancy and imagination had been stirred by family holidays to the sublime mountain regions of Wales and Scotland. 'What a land of spirit-stirring and enriching scenes and places!' he had written. He was to return to these scenes of grandeur in later years to 'recapture the thousands of vivid and tender memories', but with a different purpose. Now in his thirties, and captivated by the new science of photography, Frith set out on a series of pioneering journeys to the Nile regions that occupied him from 1856 until 1860.

INTRIGUE AND ADVENTURE

He took with him on his travels a specially-designed wicker carriage that acted as both dark-room and sleeping chamber. These far-flung journeys were packed with intrigue and adventure. In his life story, written when he was sixty-three, Frith tells of being held captive by bandits, and of fighting 'an awful midnight battle to the very point of surrender with a deadly pack of hungry, wild dogs'. Sporting flowing Arab costume, Frith arrived at Akaba by camel seventy years before Lawrence, where he encountered 'desert princes and rival sheikhs, blazing with jewel-hilted swords'.

During these extraordinary adventures he was assiduously exploring the desert regions bordering the Nile and patiently recording the antiquities and peoples with his camera. He was the first photographer to venture beyond the sixth cataract. Africa was still the mysterious 'Dark Continent', and Stanley and Livingstone's historic meeting was a decade into the future. The conditions for picture taking confound belief. He laboured for hours in his wicker dark-room in the sweltering heat of the desert, while the volatile chemicals fizzed dangerously in their trays. Often he was forced to work in remote tombs and caves where conditions were cooler. Back in London he exhibited his photographs and was 'rapturously cheered' by members of the Royal Society. His reputation as a photographer was made overnight. An eminent modern historian has likened their impact on the population of the time to that on our own generation of the first photographs taken on the surface of the moon.

VENTURE OF A LIFE-TIME

Characteristically, Frith quickly spotted the opportunity to create a new business as a specialist publisher of photographs. He lived in an era of immense and sometimes violent change. For the poor in the early part of Victoria's reign work was a drudge and the hours long, and people had precious little free time to enjoy themselves.

Most had no transport other than a cart or gig at their disposal, and had not travelled far beyond the boundaries of their own town or village. However, by the 1870s, the railways had threaded their way across the country, and Bank Holidays and half-day Saturdays had been made obligatory by Act of Parliament. All of a sudden the ordinary working man and his family were able to enjoy days out and see a little more of the world.

With characteristic business acumen, Francis Frith foresaw that these new tourists would enjoy having souvenirs to commemorate their days out. In 1860 he married Mary Ann Rosling and set out with the intention of photographing every city, town and village in Britain. For the next thirty years he travelled the country by train and by pony and trap, producing fine photographs of seaside resorts and beauty spots that were keenly bought by millions of Victorians. These prints were painstakingly pasted into family albums and pored over during the dark nights of winter, rekindling precious memories of summer excursions.

THE RISE OF FRITH & CO

Frith's studio was soon supplying retail shops all over the country. To meet the demand he gathered about him a small team of photographers, and published the work of independent artist-photographers of the calibre of Roger Fenton and Francis Bedford. In order to gain some understanding of the scale of Frith's business one only has to look at the catalogue issued by Frith & Co in 1886: it runs to some 670

pages, listing not only many thousands of views of the British Isles but also many photographs of most European countries, and China, Japan, the USA and Canada – note the sample page shown above from the hand-written *Frith & Co* ledgers detailing pictures taken. By 1890 Frith had created the greatest specialist photographic publishing company in the world, with over 2,000 outlets – more than the combined number that Boots and WH Smith have today! The picture on the right shows the *Frith & Co* display board at Ingleton in the Yorkshire Dales. Beautifully constructed with mahogany frame and gilt inserts, it could display up to a dozen local scenes.

POSTCARD BONANZA

◆

The ever-popular holiday postcard we know today took many years to develop. In 1870 the Post Office issued the first plain cards, with a pre-printed stamp on one face. In 1894 they allowed other publishers' cards to be sent through the mail with an attached adhesive halfpenny stamp. Demand grew rapidly, and in 1895 a new size of postcard was permitted called the

court card, but there was little room for illustration. In 1899, a year after Frith's death, a new card measuring 5.5 x 3.5 inches became the standard format, but it was not until 1902 that the divided back came into being, with address and message on one face and a full-size illustration on the other. *Frith & Co* were in the vanguard of postcard development, and Frith's sons Eustace and Cyril continued their father's monumental task, expanding the number of views offered to the public and recording more and more places in Britain, as the coasts and countryside were opened up to mass travel.

Francis Frith died in 1898 at his villa in Cannes, his great project still growing. The archive he created continued in business for another seventy years. By 1970 it contained over a third of a million pictures of 7,000 cities, towns and villages. The massive photographic record Frith has left to us stands as a living monument to a special and very remarkable man.

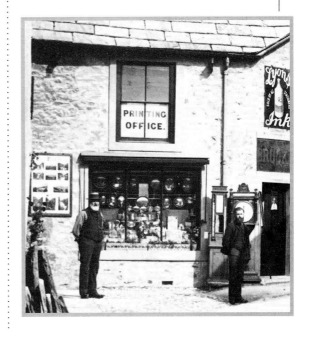

Frith's Archive: *A Unique Legacy*

FRANCIS FRITH'S legacy to us today is of immense significance and value, for the magnificent archive of evocative photographs he created provides a unique record of change in 7,000 cities, towns and villages throughout Britain over a century and more. Frith and his fellow studio photographers revisited locations many times down the years to update their views, compiling for us an enthralling and colourful pageant of British life and character.

We tend to think of Frith's sepia views of Britain as nostalgic, for most of us use them to conjure up memories of places in our own lives with which we have family associations. It often makes us forget that to Francis Frith they were records of daily life as it was actually being lived in the cities, towns and villages of his day. The Victorian age was one of great and often bewildering change for ordinary people, and though the pictures evoke an impression of slower times, life was as busy and hectic as it is today.

We are fortunate that Frith was a photographer of the people, dedicated to recording the minutiae of everyday life. For it is this sheer wealth of visual data, the painstaking chronicle of changes in dress, transport, street layouts, buildings, housing, engineering and landscape that captivates us so much today. His remarkable images offer us a powerful link with the past and with the lives of our ancestors.

TODAY'S TECHNOLOGY

Computers have now made it possible for Frith's many thousands of images to be accessed almost instantly. In the Frith archive today, each photograph is carefully 'digitised' then stored on a CD Rom. Frith archivists can locate a single photograph amongst thousands within seconds. Views can be catalogued and sorted under a variety of categories of place and content to the immediate benefit of researchers. Inexpensive reference prints can be created for them at the touch of a mouse button, and a wide range of books and other printed materials assembled and published for a wider, more general readership - in the next twelve months over a hundred Frith local history titles will be published! The

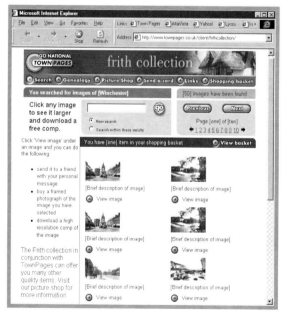

See Frith at www. francisfrith.co.uk

day-to-day workings of the archive are very different from how they were in Francis Frith's time: imagine the herculean task of sorting through eleven tons of glass negatives as Frith had to do to locate a particular sequence of pictures! Yet the archive still prides itself on maintaining the same high standards of excellence laid down by Francis Frith, including the painstaking cataloguing and indexing of every view.

It is curious to reflect on how the internet now allows researchers in America and elsewhere greater instant access to the archive than Frith himself ever enjoyed. Many thousands of individual views can be called up on screen within seconds on one of the Frith internet sites, enabling people living continents away to revisit the streets of their ancestral home town, or view places in Britain where they have enjoyed holidays. Many overseas researchers welcome the chance to view special theme selections, such as transport, sports, costume and ancient monuments.

We are certain that Francis Frith would have heartily approved of these modern developments, for he himself was always working at the very limits of Victorian photographic technology.

THE VALUE OF THE ARCHIVE TODAY

Because of the benefits brought by the computer, Frith's images are increasingly studied by social historians, by researchers into genealogy and ancestory, by architects, town planners, and by teachers and schoolchildren involved in local history projects. In addition, the archive offers every one of us a unique opportunity to examine the places where we and our families have lived and worked down the years. Immensely successful in Frith's own era, the archive is now, a century and more on, entering a new phase of popularity.

THE PAST IN TUNE WITH THE FUTURE

Historians consider the Francis Frith Collection to be of prime national importance. It is the only archive of its kind remaining in private ownership and has been valued at a million pounds. However, this figure is now rapidly increasing as digital technology enables more and more people around the world to enjoy its benefits.

Francis Frith's archive is now housed in an historic timber barn in the beautiful village of Teffont in Wiltshire. Its founder would not recognize the archive office as it is today. In place of the many thousands of dusty boxes containing glass plate negatives and an all-pervading odour of photographic chemicals, there are now ranks of computer screens. He would be amazed to watch his images travelling round the world at unimaginable speeds through network and internet lines.

The archive's future is both bright and exciting. Francis Frith, with his unshakeable belief in making photographs available to the greatest number of people, would undoubtedly approve of what is being done today with his lifetime's work. His photographs, depicting our shared past, are now bringing pleasure and enlightenment to millions around the world a century and more after his death.

THE DORSET COAST
– *An Introduction*

TO JOURNEY along the coastline of Dorset is to travel back in time, for few landscapes in England show as much evidence of either their geological origins, or the multitude of civilisations that have lived and worked upon the fields and clifftops, as this ancient countryside does. Dorset is a county of rolling downlands, deep wooded valleys, and some of the most picturesque towns and villages to be found in the south of Britain.

This is a territory familiar to millions of people throughout the world who may not ever have visited it, for it is immortalised in the novels and poems of Thomas Hardy, Jane Austen, John Fowles and the Powys Brothers; it has also been pictured by hundreds of artists of all abilities. For this is a land that cries out for interpretation: its lonely coves, hilltop forts and tranquil downs and meadows seem to throw out stories, characters and scenic beauty in a way that inspires the artistic mind. The photographic essays of the Frith family capture this mood in all its subtleties.

The Dorset Coast Path follows the coastline from Lyme Regis to Poole, and a walk along it, with suitable diversions inland, is the best way to experience the county as the Friths would have known it. The waves still beat on the shingle shore, curlews still cry above the marshlands, and the sheep still graze on the downs. This is an ancient land, old when the Romans came. Invaders, journeymen workers, merchants, sailors, rebels and artists have all come and gone; and now locals and tourists alike delight in this old county. The Dorset Coast, once visited, lives forever in the memory.

WEST DORSET - THE COAST OF FOSSILS

MOST VISITORS agree that the best way to approach the West Dorset coast is from further west, along the road out of Devon that plunges downhill and into Dorset towards Lyme Regis. Suddenly a great vista opens across Lyme Bay, revealing the strangely beautiful coloured cliffs around Charmouth, then the great height of Golden Cap, and then Portland beyond. Motorists have been known to bring their cars to a sudden halt, so captivated have they been by this extensive view.

Lyme Regis clings to the valley of the tiny River Lim and the hills above as though it has somehow grown organically out of the landscape. Lyme cries out to be painted or photographed - and often is. In recent years it has become the favoured location of film-makers who have transformed it back in time to play its earlier self in productions of Jane Austen's 'Persuasion' and John Fowles' 'The French Lieutenant's Woman', both of which are set in the town.

Both novels have had a weird effect on the town, their characters becoming as much a part of Lyme's history as the Duke of Monmouth, who began his 1685 rebellion there, or Mary Anning, who boosted the science of palaeontology through her seaside discoveries. Tourists walk on to The Cobb, that unique harbour wall that beats back the English Channel, to see the very spot where Charles Ryder first beheld Sarah Woodruff in Fowles' novel, or the hazardous flight of steps that Louisa Musgrove foolishly jumped off in Austen's masterpiece - as though for all the world they were real events.

The great line of cliffs between here and Abbotsbury are unstable and rock falls are common. In recent years the headlands between Lyme and Charmouth have fallen on many occasions, causing a considerable amount of coastal erosion, but producing a generous crop of fossils with every fall - to the delight of the fossil hunters who can often be seen strolling along the beaches, hammers in hand. Lyme had its first fossil shop a century ago and several now thrive in the town.

Mary Anning brought Lyme into the fossil hunter's spotlight with her discovery of an ichthyosaur on the beach near Charmouth in 1811, winning scientific acclaim and changing her society's preconceptions about the origins of life on earth. This discovery was remarkable in itself, but astonishing given that Mary was the barely-educated daughter of the local carpenter. She was rightly feted by her contemporaries, for Mary Anning was one of the most astonishing women of the 19th century and deserves to be much better recognised and honoured in the nation's history.

The coast from Charmouth onwards is punctuated by a series of coves, with attractive hamlets and villages beyond. Charmouth and Chideock spill down towards the sea from the old coaching route that has now become a busy tourist road. Here Saxon and Dane tussled for possession of the airy downlands, and Charles II hid on his escape to the coast after the Battle of Worcester in 1651. These are smuggler's settlements; it is not difficult to conjure up images of pack-ponies carrying casks of brandy up the steep lanes and tracks leading from what must have been very lonely beaches.

Bridport is a bustling market town to which most of the population of West Dorset seems to descend on market days. It is not difficult to imagine Thomas Hardy, who often cycled this way, taking note of the characters that would come to the town and immortalising them in his great series of Wessex novels.

LYME REGIS 1890 27342
Lyme Regis, seen here from the heights of Timber Hill, is situated at the westernmost end of Dorset. Walking through the fields and cliffs of Lyme the visitor can never be quite sure whether he or she is in Dorset or neighbouring Devon. Some residents at the far end of town are Devonians, while the rest are 'Dorset Good and True'.

LYME REGIS, GENERAL VIEW 1890 27343

This part of the Dorset coastline is very ancient and extremely unstable. Here we see a view of the town from the cliffs known as The Spittles. Much of the clifftop nearby has long since crashed down into the sea.

LYME REGIS, BROAD STREET 1905 L121001

Visitors approaching from Devon descend this steep hill to the sea at Lyme. Broad Street is the town's most fashionable shopping street, though the busy traffic of today prevents dogs lying down in the road!

LYME REGIS
Broad Street 1900 45242
Looking back up Broad Street one can see a great variety of inns and hotels. Famous visitors to Lyme have included Daniel Defoe, Mary Mitford, Jane Austen, Alfred Tennyson and Beatrix Potter. Their visits have resulted in Lyme being widely mentioned in literature. More recently, John Fowles immortalised the town in his famous novel 'The French Lieutenant's Woman'.

LYME REGIS, THE SMITHY 1909 61633a
Lyme Regis' most famous blacksmith's forge stood in Broad Street, more or less on the site of the present Woolworth's store. The great American painter Whistler immortalised the forge in his renowned painting 'The Master-Smith of Lyme Regis', when he visited the town in 1895.

LYME REGIS, THE COBB 1906 54528

The massive sea wall and jetty known as The Cobb is probably Lyme Regis' most famous feature, familiar to all who remember the actress Meryl Streep wandering along it on a stormy day in the film version of 'The French Lieutenant's Woman'. Its author, John Fowles, has lived in Lyme for many years and is one of a long line of writers to feature this landmark in their writings.

LYME REGIS, THE HARBOUR 1892 31308

When the nearby harbour of Axmouth fell into disuse after a cliff-fall in the 12th century, the only alternative was to extend the harbour at Lyme Regis. 'There is not any harbour like it in the world', the topographer Roger North exclaimed in 1582, as he described the new docks at Lyme. By the Victorian age, hundreds of ships were trading in and out of Lyme every year.

LYME REGIS, THE HARBOUR 1912 65039

LYME REGIS
The Harbour 1912
In the Middle Ages local merchants established a cloth and wool trade between Lyme and the French port of Morlaix, which prospered in spite of the long years of war between the two countries. Perhaps Lyme's most famous ship was the 'Revenge', commanded by Sir Francis Drake during his battle with the Spanish Armada in 1588, and later by Sir Richard Grenville.

LYME REGIS
Sherborne Lane 1907
At this time the Crown and Anchor Inn, the large building at the foot of the hill, was still open and a focus for community life in Lyme Regis. This is by far the oldest part of the town, having been built on land given to Sherborne Abbey by the Wessex king Cynewulf in 774.

LYME REGIS, SHERBORNE LANE 1907 58099

LYME REGIS, THE COBB 1912 65040
This fine study of the Granny's Teeth steps on the Cobb shows the setting of the incident in Jane Austen's novel 'Persuasion' where Louisa Musgrove falls off the wall. Jane Austen visited the town and adored the setting, capturing her enthusiasm in her novel. 'The young people were all wild to see Lyme', she wrote as her characters approached the town.

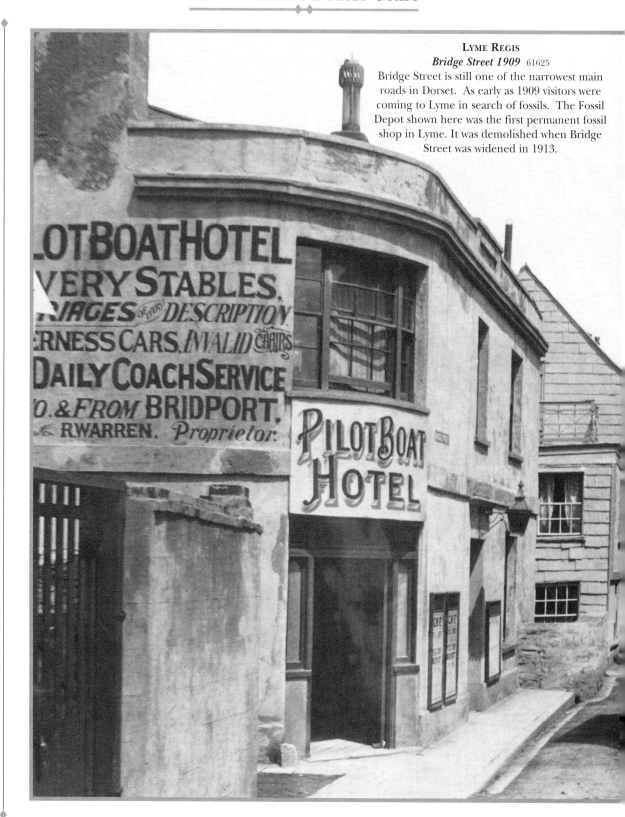

LYME REGIS
Bridge Street 1909 61625
Bridge Street is still one of the narrowest main roads in Dorset. As early as 1909 visitors were coming to Lyme in search of fossils. The Fossil Depot shown here was the first permanent fossil shop in Lyme. It was demolished when Bridge Street was widened in 1913.

LYME REGIS, STREET 1892 31311

The old tracks from the neighbouring village of Uplyme are the original routes into the town before the construction of the present road along the coast. Down the tracks packhorses would have brought wool and cloth to the harbour, and rebels would have wearily tramped to join the Duke of Monmouth's army, which gathered in the town in 1685. Jane Austen probably caught her first glimpse of the town from one of these old routes.

LYME REGIS, THE VIADUCT 1903 50253

Lyme Regis was relatively late in having the advantage of its own railway line; its station opened in 1903. Cannington Viaduct, at Uplyme, was one of the first railway bridges to be made out of concrete. The railway link to the town was severed in the 1960s.

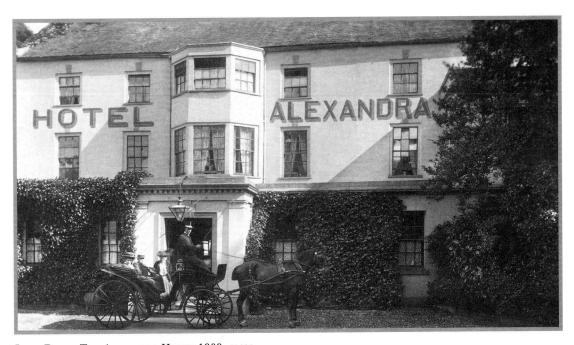

LYME REGIS, THE ALEXANDRA HOTEL 1909 61631

The Alexandra Hotel was established in 1888 and still welcomes guests today. The building was originally the home of William Pinney MP in the days of ancient boroughs, when Lyme had its own representative at Westminster. The extensive grounds are now part of the public gardens above Marine Parade.

LYME REGIS
The Victoria Hotel 1907 58092
Lyme Regis became a fashionable resort two hundred
years ago; in the intervening years a number of fine
luxury hotels have been built to cope with the increasing
number of visitors who come for the bracing air and wild
romantic scenery.

CHARMOUTH, THE VILLAGE 1890 27380
Charmouth village stretches up the long hillside on the western side of the river Char. Few have described the scene as well as Jane Austen in 'Persuasion': 'Charmouth, with its high grounds and extensive sweeps of country, and, still more, its sweet retired bay, backed by dark cliffs, where fragments of low rock among the sands make it the happiest spot for watching the flow of the tide; for sitting in unwearied contemplation'.

CHARMOUTH, STREET VIEW 1898 27382

Charmouth was a notable settlement even in Saxon times when two Saxon kings, Egbert and Ethelwulf, fought the Danes nearby. A later king, Charles II, hid here briefly during his escape from the Battle of Worcester. The heart of the village is the steep main street, lined with some splendid bow-windowed cottages.

CHARMOUTH, THE VILLAGE 1922 72790

Once on the high road between Axminster and Bridport, Charmouth has now been bypassed, but even so the traffic up the steep hill out of the village will never be as quiet as on the peaceful day pictured here.

CHARMOUTH, THE RIVER CHAR c1960 C66069

CHARMOUTH
The River Char c1960

The beach at Charmouth is a mecca for geologists and fossil hunters, and explanatory walks take place from the heritage centre by the mouth of the Char. It was near here that Mary Anning discovered the remains of an ichthyosaurus in 1811, helping to launch the new science of palaeontology and changing the course of scientific thought.

◆

CHIDEOCK
The Village 1912

Chideock, usually pronounced without the 'e', stands rooted in history along the line of an old stagecoach route. It was for many years the haunt of Dorset smugglers, who landed their cargoes on the nearby beach of Seatown.

CHIDEOCK, THE VILLAGE 1912 65079

CHIDEOCK, THE VILLAGE 1912 65080
Set in a landscape of rolling hills and ancient ridgeways, the charming cottages of Chideock witnessed some of the fiercest fighting in the English Civil War, as parliamentarian troops from the besieged Lyme Regis rode out to raid the enclosing Royalist army.

NETHERBURY
The Village 1912 65068
A pastoral scene which might have come from a
novel by Thomas Hardy. Harvesters work the fields
within the shadow of Netherbury Church in the
last peaceful years before the Great War.

EYPE, THE BEACH 1930 83371

Eype in the days before it was invaded by caravans and the steady influx of tourists who now descend to the beach at Eype Mouth. In days gone by, this wild stretch of coastline would have been known to few except fishermen, shepherds and smugglers.

WEST BAY, THE QUAY 1897 40081

West Bay is the small port of the neighbouring town of Bridport. The River Brit, which gives the larger town its name, is held back by a series of sluices and released at low tide. The swell between the piers as the great waves of Lyme Bay wash into the harbour entrance is an awesome sight.

WEST BAY, THE HARBOUR 1930 83355
West Bay only acquired its name in the 1880s when the railway was brought down to its picturesque harbour. The larger sailing vessels of late Victorian days have gone, but fishing boats still leave the harbour to bring home their catch, when the swell of the channel allows them to pass through the narrow harbour entrance.

WEST BAY
General View 1930 83349
West Bay has now become the setting for a popular television series, 'Harbour Lights', which has brought many more tourists to the village. Attempts by the Victorians to turn West Bay into a leading holiday resort never quite worked, though a great many holiday flats have been built in recent years. However, it is a mecca for day-trippers.

WEST BAY, THE PROMENADE 1930 83352

Away from the great cliffs of Lyme and Charmouth, the coastline begins to sweep down to sea-level near West Bay, until the land meets the sea in the long shingle bank of Chesil Beach and the Fleet, a fresh-water lake.

BRIDPORT, FROM ALLINGTON HILL 1897 40068

As long ago as the reign of Edward the Confessor, Bridport was a town of considerable importance, boasting over a hundred dwellings, a priory of monks and its own mint. As its name implies, it was once the port on the River Brit or Bredy, though the original harbour silted up long ago, forcing the construction of the new anchorage at West Bay.

BRIDPORT, SOUTH STREET 1897 40070
From early times, Bridport was famous for the growing of hemp and the manufacture of rope. In the small streets and alleyways off South Street, the old rope-walks can still be seen. Much of the cordage for Royal Navy vessels was produced in and around Bridport.

BRIDPORT, EAST STREET 1897 40074
East Street and West Street form part of the old coaching route between Exeter and Dorchester. The wide road shows the importance of this route to the town. The wide pavements are said to have been constructed to facilitate rope and net making outside the inhabitants' houses.

BRIDPORT
East Street 1904 52756
Here we see the junction of East Street and South
Street, with the Georgian town hall jutting out
onto the highway on the right. Market stalls still
line the main street on market days, attracting
customers from all over West Dorset.

BRIDPORT, WEST STREET 1913 65643

Ropes were made in the alleyways around West Street. The old expression 'to be stabbed by a Bridport dagger' meant to be hanged by a rope made in the town.

BOTHENHAMPTON, THE VILLAGE 1904 52767

Once a village in its own right, standing on the slopes above the River Bredy, Bothenhampton has now become a suburb of Bridport. It is best known for the beauty of the architecture of its two churches: the ancient building has been sympathetically restored, and the newer place of worship has four impressive stone arches which rise high above the congregation.

BURTON BRADSTOCK, THE VILLAGE 1930 83365
King Henry I gave the village and living of Burton Bradstock to the great Normandy abbey at Caen in exchange for the royal regalia of William the Conqueror, which the monks at Caen claimed had been left to them by the dying king. Thus the crown jewels were redeemed by the gift of this tiny village.

Weymouth and Portland - The Thomas Hardy Coast

WEYMOUTH was one of the earliest holiday resorts on England's southern coast, thanks both to its happy geographical location and the patronage of King George III, who came here to sea bathe on the recommendation of his doctors, and who is commemorated by a dreadful statue and a rather fetching hill-carving.

Fashionable Georgian society flocked in his wake to the otherwise peaceful village, as did Victorian gentlefolk. But for the ascendancy of Brighton, nearer to London and patronised by King George's elegant son the Prince Regent, Weymouth might have continued to be the epicentre of social fashion, a kind of Bath-by-the-sea. Happily, democracy prevailed and the town opened its welcoming arms to the many rather than the few - although it never felt the need to stoop to downmarket tourist attractions as a way of luring this new clientele.

Weymouth is made by its setting; the graceful conformation of Weymouth Bay has commonly been compared to the Bay of Naples, and rightly so. The town stands on a narrow spit of land between this grand stretch of water and the harbour and the beautiful Radipole Lake. Birdwatchers flock to the area for the sheer variety of the birdlife - nature tourism is the rising star all along this coast. Beyond Weymouth, on the journey inland, are the great Dorset downs, the massive hillfort of Maiden Castle, and the county capital, Dorchester - Thomas Hardy's 'Casterbridge'. Such historic and literary associations have made the town a popular touring centre for those holidaymakers who wish to do more than sit on Weymouth's sheltered beaches all day.

Weymouth is a seaside town in every sense of the word, for no street is more than a few minutes stroll from the water. This accessibility to the Channel has added to Weymouth's importance as a port, for the harbour is the starting point for the thousands of tourists who cross to the Channel Islands and Continent each year. This journeying was not always quite so peaceful in its intent; generations of local seamen left Weymouth in earlier times to raid the French and Spanish coasts, and Nelson's navy used Weymouth Bay as an anchorage from which to blockade the Continent during the Napoleonic Wars. British, French and American troops quietly slipped out of Weymouth in June 1944 to participate in the D-Day landings. The export of holidaymakers and the import of Jersey tomatoes seems peaceful by comparison.

Much of the old naval harbour nestling to the east of Portland can still be seen, though its role in maritime affairs has diminished. The helicopter training section at Portland, whose aircraft were once a familiar sight around the bay, lowered the White Ensign in 1999 and its sailors marched away. But the visitor can still explore the old fortifications, such as around the Nothe Gardens, which once played such a vital part in the defence of the anchorage.

The Isle of Portland guards Weymouth Bay from the worst excesses of the south westerly gales. It is, of course, mis-named - for a spit of land connects Portland to the mainland, making it a peninsula. Thomas Hardy was impressed and called the Isle 'England's Gibraltar' and featured it in his writings as the 'Isle of Slingers'. At first sight, Portland can be forbidding, with its functional housing, prison and huge quarries. Many are repelled by the Isle, finding it ugly and industrial, but it has both grace and majesty as it sits defiantly out in the English Channel, riding the waves as proudly as a battleship, visible on clear days from distant coastlines in Devon and Hampshire. Given the scale of the quarrying, and the ubiquitous presence of Portland Stone in buildings throughout the world, the wonder is that there is any of the island left. Such an environment bred strong characters who had the choice of two hard livings, quarrying and fishing. It is a testimony to their capacity for hard work and their commitment to this rocky home that any communities survived here at all, and that the natives did not desert the place in search of an easier living elsewhere.

Beyond Portland is a long stretch of lonely coastline leading east to Swanage. Some enterprising tourist authority really should label this spectacular shore the 'Hardy Coast', for it lives in its earlier existence in that

author's novels and poems, and not that much has changed.

Lulworth Cove, for all its popularity, is the joy of this coastline, its perfect circle seemingly reproduced on every other postcard and painting on sale in Dorset. It was beloved by poets such as Hardy and Rupert Brooke, and a century earlier John Keats found solace there before departing to Rome and death. Even the nearby tank training areas have scarcely spoiled its tranquillity, though most tourists feel a deep sadness when visiting the ruins of the nearby village of Tyneham, where the local people were evicted by the military during the Second World War and never allowed to return. It is worth a visit on non-firing days to see a part of Dorset lost in time, beautiful but heartbreaking.

There are other lost coves and wild shorelines, but many are only accessible on foot, thank goodness! If the visitor wishes to experience the heart of Dorset, and to appreciate the landscape as it was known and understood by all those famous poets, artists and photographers like the Friths, then a walk along the coastal footpath is a must.

WEYMOUTH, SANDSFOOT CASTLE AND THE ISLE OF PORTLAND 1904 52869
Sandsfoot Castle was built by King Henry VIII to guard the sea-lanes between Weymouth and Portland. It was described by the Tudor topographer Leland as 'a right goodlie and warlyke castle'. The castle changed hands several times during the English Civil War, before finally falling into ruin in the 1700s.

WEYMOUTH, THE NOTHE GARDENS 1909 61591

Weymouth's Nothe Gardens are beautifully situated on a headland overlooking the Isle of Portland and are the site of Nothe Fort, built to guard the huge naval harbour between the mainland and the Isle. At the time this view was taken Nothe Fort was equipped with quick-firing guns and could accommodate a battalion of soldiers.

WEYMOUTH, THE JERSEY BOAT 1890 27318

The trade with the Channel Islands and France began soon after the Norman Conquest. It is likely that the inhabitants of inland villages such as Wyke Regis and Melcombe Regis moved nearer the sea to take advantage of these new markets for goods, establishing the present town and harbour at Weymouth.

WEYMOUTH
The Harbour 1904 52861
A fine sailing vessel is moored near Weymouth Bridge.
The heyday of sail was almost over; steam vessels were
replacing the ocean-going ships, but some sailing
vessels continued to trade from Weymouth well into the
1920s. A renaissance of interest in sailing ships has
resulted in many modern-day sailing vessels mooring
around the ancient Dorset port.

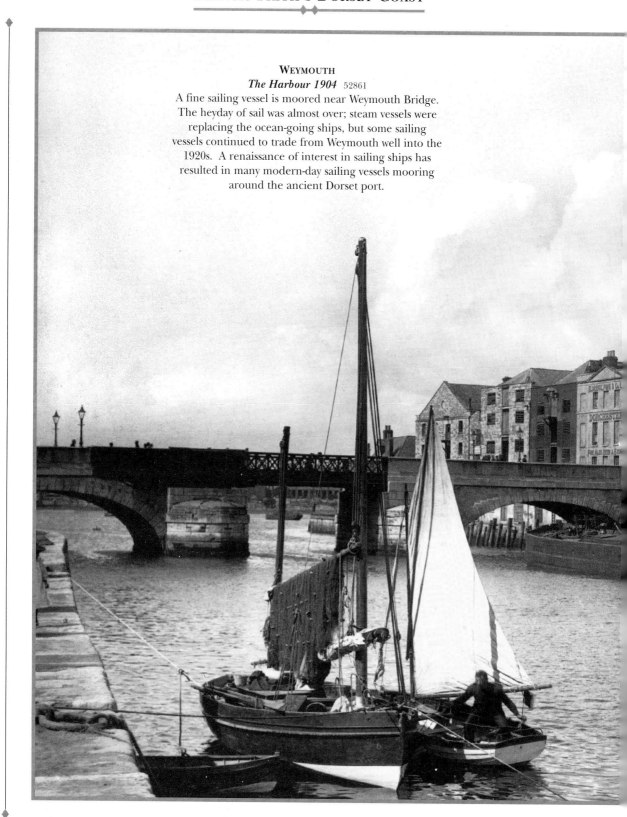

WEYMOUTH, THE HARBOUR 34539

Although now best known as a holiday resort, Weymouth remains an important port and ferry terminal, maintaining the link between England and the Continent established so long ago. Many of the troopships for the Normandy invasion of June 1944 set sail from Weymouth and neighbouring Dorset ports.

WEYMOUTH, THE HARBOUR 1898 41114

After Weymouth harbour was dredged and improved in 1888, larger ships joined the trade routes between the town and foreign ports. By the 1950s, 700,000,000 tomatoes were brought into the port and 150,000 passengers were transported to the Continent in an average year.

WEYMOUTH, THE HARBOUR 1898 41112
A paddle steamer lies moored at the harbour wall. The first steam-paddle driven vessels, the 'Ivanhoe' and 'Warspite', arrived in Weymouth as early as 1827. The ship pictured here is probably one of their successors, built by the famous Lairds yard at Birkenhead in the 1890s.

WEYMOUTH, THE PARADE 1898 41119
Weymouth became popular as a seaside resort thanks to the patronage of King George III, who came to bathe here for the good of his health. As the king plunged into the waves a brass band, discreetly hidden in a bathing machine, played 'God Save the King'! King George is commemorated by a statue in the town and a carved chalk figure on the hills nearby.

WEYMOUTH
Beach Show 1899 43853x
An ancient guidebook stressed the health benefits of a
holiday in Weymouth: 'Weymouth is much more open
than the majority of seaside resorts, and is almost
surrounded by salt water. This results in an air largely
impregnated with ozone and, with the ever-changing tide,
ensures a constantly renewed atmosphere'.

WEYMOUTH, THE ESPLANADE 1899 43852

Weymouth, unlike many south coast resorts, faces east; it is therefore possible to sit on hot sunny days without the glare of the afternoon sun in the face. This accounted for the popularity of the long beach and the Esplanade.

WEYMOUTH, THE PARADE 1904 52857

The Parade was built in Georgian times as the fashionable residential quarter of the town. Near here, members of the royal family would stay during and after the reign of George III. In the far distance is the spire of St. John's church, a very prominent landmark from out at sea.

WEYMOUTH
The Pavilion 1909
At the entrance to Weymouth Pier stands the Pavilion Theatre, pictured here the year after it opened. The Pavilion quickly eclipsed the other small theatres around the town, offering a variety of plays all the year round. It was constructed with a seating capacity of 1100.

WEYMOUTH
The Pier and Pavilion 1909
The Esplanade winds around to the Pier and Pavilion Theatre, a favourite stroll for the Edwardian visitor. The pier at this time was 1,050 feet long, and a favoured location for watching the steamers come in and out. The Edwardian visitor would have paid two pence (old currency) to walk to the end of the pier.

WEYMOUTH, THE PAVILION 1909 61594

WEYMOUTH, THE PIER AND PAVILION 1909 61589

WEYMOUTH
The Sands 1909 61597
Sea-bathers are gathered in front of the Jubilee
Clock. Visitors then would probably have paid
63 shillings (£3.15) to stay full board at one of the
better hotels in the town, and anything from
8 shillings (40 pence) if they lodged at one of
the poorest.

WEYMOUTH, THE SANDS 1909 61596
Much of modern Weymouth is in fact in the old Borough of Melcombe Regis, which in older times was the larger habitation of the two. For many years, the old town of Weymouth thrived on the brewing of beer rather than on tourism.

WEYMOUTH, NEW KURSAAL 1913 65654
The Kursaal in Alexandra Gardens was erected as a venue for musical soirees and other social events. On summer evenings, the Weymouth Municipal Band would give a concert, aided by local singers. The performances would be repeated on three mornings a week.

WEYMOUTH, THE SANDS 1918 68116

It was the early use of bathing machines that made Weymouth such a popular resort for sea bathing. The larger machines ran down into the water on rails and consisted of a number of cubicles. Affluent visitors would hire a single machine for themselves.

WEYMOUTH, THE PARADE 1923 73953

Weymouth is constantly likened to the Bay of Naples for the beauty of its setting and the fine curves of its coastline. During the depression of the 1920s many tourists holidayed at home instead of going abroad, laying the foundations for Weymouth's rise as a modern holiday resort.

WEYMOUTH, THE PUNCH AND JUDY SHOW c1955 W76196
Some scenes at the seaside never seem to change. From early Victorian times Punch and Judy shows moved away from the fairgrounds and streets and on to the beach in pursuit of lucrative new audiences. This photograph shows a full-size Punch and Judy booth, much wider than many of the booths used today.

WEYMOUTH, THE PARADE 1923 73950

Weymouth remained a popular escape from the horrors of the First World War and the resort coped well during those lean and dark years. In the war's aftermath tourists, many just glad to be alive, enjoyed traditional seaside holidays to the full.

PORTLAND, CHESIL BANK C1875 8064

The Isle of Portland is more properly a peninsula, which the novelist Thomas Hardy described as 'The Gibraltar of Wessex'. Situated at the end of the long sweep of Chesil Beach, Portland gives shelter to the westerly approaches of Weymouth Bay and is visible for a great many miles up and down the English Channel.

PORTLAND, CHESIL BEACH 1890 27328

Chesil Beach is a great ridge of shingle eight miles long, with a lagoon of brackish water between it and the mainland. The stones tend to be larger at one end of the beach than the other. John Meade Faulkner immortalised the locality in his famous smuggling novel 'Moonfleet'.

PORTLAND, THE BREAKWATER 1890 27333

The great breakwaters around the eastern shores of Portland entirely enclose Portland harbour. They were constructed in the second half of the 19th century to enhance the naval port that had developed over the previous centuries. The older breakwater took twenty-three years to build and cost over a million pounds - a considerable amount of money at that time.

PORTLAND
Castleton from Chesil Beach 1894

Castleton, Fortuneswell and Chesil now form a large urban settlement where Portland meets the mainland. At the time this photograph was taken, they were three discrete settlements, overlooking the great naval base in one direction and being overlooked by the great convict prison from the other.

◆

PORTLAND
1894

Portland stone is renowned throughout the world as a prime building material. Sir Christopher Wren used this durable material for St. Paul's Cathedral. Apart from private family-run quarries, much of the stone was broken by convicts from the nearby prison. Here we can see convicts being marched in strict order for a day's work with pickaxe and crowbar.

PORTLAND, CASTLETON FROM CHESIL BEACH 1894   34549

PORTLAND 1894   34553

PORTLAND
Fortune's Well 1894 34550
Portland's main town of Fortuneswell grew up, as the
name implies, around a well, as did most of the
Portland settlements. A supply of pure water would
have been essential on this barren rock, almost
surrounded by salt water.

PORTLAND, PENNSYLVANIA COVE 1898 41145

The area of Portland known as Pennsylvania was named by James Penn, Governor of the island in Napoleonic times, in honour of his grandfather William Penn, founder of the American state. This photograph shows just how rocky Portland is, and why it became such an important centre for the quarrying industry.

PORTLAND, THE PULPIT ROCK 1898 41150

Portland Bill juts out into the English Channel at the southernmost point of the island. The Pulpit Rock is just one of the many unusual and dramatic rock formations in the vicinity.

PORTLAND, THE LIGHTHOUSE C.1955 P91022
Portland lighthouse was opened in the early years of the 20th century to replace two ancient lighthouses that once stood nearby. Portland has always presented a danger to shipping; Captain John Wordsworth, brother of the poet, drowned here with 200 shipmates when his ship the Abergavenny sank in 1805.

UPWEY - *The Wishing Well 1923* 73960
The village of Upwey stands on the high road between Weymouth and Dorchester and features in Thomas Hardy's novel 'The Trumpet-Major'. The famous wishing well was a favourite day out for early visitors to Weymouth, who would taste the water and think of their heart's desire. A shack nearby provided simple refreshments, and the tourists would sit on the surrounding benches.

LULWORTH, BISHOP'S COTTAGE 1894 34563

The villages of West and East Lulworth now stand adjacent to vast military firing ranges, though fortunately they never suffered the fate of nearby Tyneham, which was taken by the army during the Second World War and never returned to its villagers.

LULWORTH COVE, WEST POINT 1894 34575

A perfect natural harbour, Lulworth Cove has been hollowed out by the swirling waters of the English Channel into its present almost circular form, creating one of the most distinctive bays on the coast of southern England.

LULWORTH COVE 1894 34569

By the end of the 19th century, Lulworth Cove was already attracting a great number of visitors, determined to see this unique Dorset landmark. However, when this photograph was taken the area and its people still revolved around traditional industries such as farming and fishing.

LULWORTH COVE, STAIR HOLE 1894 34576
Stair Hole, where the downlands of Dorset meet the sea, is hollowed out by vast caverns, many used by smugglers for centuries. The South West Way Coastal Footpath, once an old coastguard route, gives excellent views over these wild headlands and coves.

LULWORTH COVE 1903 49137
The beauty of Lulworth Cove has always attracted writers and artists. John Keats spent some of his last days in England here, as did Rupert Brooke who returned several times before sailing away to the First World War. Thomas Hardy immortalised the cove in poems and novels, while artists' views of 'the perfect circle' are on sale in many Dorset galleries and gift shops.

Purbeck and Poole
- Along a Saxon Shore

PURBECK, like Portland, is not an island at all, but a beautiful and fascinating peninsula in what used to be the south eastern-most corner of Dorset before the addition of Bournemouth and Christchurch. But for a freak of geological activity, Purbeck might have become a true island in the English Channel.

Swanage, the only major settlement in the Isle, dominates Purbeck's coastline. It is a holiday resort that seems unable to decide whether to appeal to the masses or to the more exclusive visitor. It does both well, and has also managed to retain its charm. A Georgian gentleman, one William Morton Pitt, purchased the estate in the 1820s, and tried to develop the town as a popular watering place in emulation of nearby Weymouth. He was ahead of his time, for it was difficult to gain access to the little town except by sea. The coming of the railway in 1885 transformed Swanage's fortunes, not only to the benefit of the tourist trade but to the quarriers of Purbeck Stone, who found an easy way to transport their product throughout Britain.

This coast was much favoured by the Saxon kings of Wessex, and the area features in the Anglo-Saxon Chronicle. Alfred the Great defeated the Danes in a great naval battle off Durlston Head in 877, and the area can tell many tales of skirmish and battle throughout England's history.

Following in the footsteps of the earliest visitors eastwards along the coast, the Saxon shore brings us to Studland. This picturesque Dorset village has a fine beach and is surrounded by the remnants of the great Dorset heathland, which must have been considerable and forbidding in Saxon times. Studland remains one of those pretty English villages that have survived against the odds. The joy of Studland is its rare combination of picturesque buildings, woodland and heath. The National Trust fortunately owns much of it, and Studland Heath is now a nature reserve. The church is pure Saxon, though remodelled by the Normans, and attracts church enthusiasts from around the world. Many come to see the grave of Sergeant William Lawrence, who lies buried in the churchyard alongside his French wife Clothilde; at rest after long years of battle alongside Wellington in Spain and at Waterloo.

Poole Harbour is claimed by some to be the finest natural anchorage in the world, and is much loved by yachtsmen. These were disputed waters during the long sea and land war between Saxon and Dane; it is not difficult, even on the busiest days, to imagine a Viking longship slipping between the islands and mudbanks, seeking out Saxon settlements to raid. Nature thrives here; Brownsea Island is a nature reserve, owned by the National Trust. Almost a century ago,

young army officer Robert Baden Powell brought a party of boys to camp there, fired them with a love of nature and outdoor life, and thus sowed the seeds leading to the formation of the Boy Scout movement.

Poole itself was the largest settlement in Dorset until some unkind bureaucrat filched Bournemouth from the neighbouring county of Hampshire and extended Dorset's boundary beyond Christchurch. Poole was old when the Romans settled; it has a proud history of mercantile adventuring, its ships sailing all over the world in search of trade and new places to explore. The older parts of this large town cluster around the ancient quays, and a great deal of fine architecture remains, thanks to stalwart local defenders.

SWANAGE, FROM DARLASTON CASTLE 1892 31354
This fine view of the Undercliff and Peveril Point from Durlston Head shows the western approaches to Swanage, which lies in the next bay. Near here, King Alfred the Great defeated the Danes in one of the earliest of all British naval battles in the year 877.

SWANAGE
The Globe 1894

The Globe at Swanage was carved out of a great mass of Portland Stone, ten feet in diameter and forty tons in weight. The Globe is positioned to represent the position of the earth in space, with nearby benches marking the points of the compass.

◆

SWANAGE
The Bay 1894

Thomas Hardy admirably described Swanage in his novel 'The Hand of Ethelberta' as '...a seaside village, lying snugly within two headlands as between a finger and thumb. Everybody in the parish who was not a boatman was a quarrier, unless he were the gentleman who owned half the property and had been a quarryman, or the other gentleman who owned the other half, and had been to sea'.

SWANAGE, THE GLOBE 1894   34607

SWANAGE, THE BAY 1894   34602

SWANAGE
From The Pier 1897 40301
Swanage Pier is really a jetty, 28 feet wide and 1,400 feet long. When this photograph was taken, the pier would have been mostly used to give access to the great number of coastal steamers that anchored alongside each day to carry passengers to towns like Weymouth and Bournemouth.

SWANAGE, THE STATION YARD 1897 40303

The Isle of Purbeck, that great peninsula sprawling eastwards into Poole harbour, is riddled with quarries. The railway station at Swanage was used to bring the stone to ships for transportation around the world. The industry has declined in importance since this photograph was taken.

SWANAGE, FROM THE COASTGUARD STATION 1897 40308

Swanage may get its name from Swene's Wic, the Bay of Swene, perhaps commemorating the naval battle between Saxons and Danes in 877. The Isle of Purbeck was a great stronghold for the Wessex Saxons for three centuries.

SWANAGE, THE COASTGUARD STATION 1897 40310

For hundreds of years, the nearness of Purbeck to the coast of France meant that smuggling was a major industry; smuggled goods would often be hidden in the caves and quarries of the Isle. Prominent coastguard stations with clear Channel views were built along the coast as a deterrent, such as this one at Swanage. Coastal watching also helped to safeguard small boats caught out in wild water and uncertain tides.

SWANAGE, TILLY WHIM 1899 43775

Tilly Whim Caves, on the coast west of Swanage, are a strange mixture of natural erosion and quarrying. Tilly Whim was an attraction noted by early guidebook writers, who nevertheless deplored the graffiti carved into the rocks by Victorian visitors.

SWANAGE, THE PROMENADE 1925 78791
On Swanage's mixed bathing beach tents were provided for changing and preserving the modesty of visitors. Men were charged three old pence and ladies four old pence for the privilege of using the facilities, though bathers could pitch their own tent for two shillings and sixpence (15 pence) a week.

SWANAGE
The Beach 1918

The coming of the railway brought tourists to Swanage in greater numbers than ever before, attracted by the scenery as much as the sandy beach and gentle tides. This view shows a world a long way from the horrific war being waged across the water in France.

SWANAGE
Station Road 1925

Station Road was probably the first view of the town for most tourists, leading as it does from the railway to the sea front.

It was a popular street for local shoppers, with a large selection of family retailers, though even as long ago as 1925 shops were catering for tourists with beach goods and souvenirs.

SWANAGE, THE BEACH 1918 68090

SWANAGE, STATION ROAD 1925 78794

STUDLAND, THE BAY 1899 43778

The journey to Studland Bay was probably the favourite excursion for tourists from Swanage, who could either get there by walking along the cliff tops or by taking a carriage or charabanc along the lanes, admiring the views across to Bournemouth, the Needles and the Isle of Wight as they went.

STUDLAND, THE BEACH 1925 78796

The attraction of Studland is not only the splendid beach and picturesque coastal scenery, but also the wild heathland all around the village. Studland Heath is now a National Nature Reserve, famous for its variety of birdlife.

STUDLAND, THE BEACH 1925 78797
Studland's most famous resident was Sergeant William Lawrence, who fought with Wellington in Spain and at Waterloo, before spending his retirement running an inn in the village with his French wife Clothilde Clairet. The old soldier and his wife would often be seen strolling hand in hand on Studland Beach and are now buried together in the village churchyard.

POOLE, THE HARBOUR 1900 46089

The town of Poole grew up around the older quays of the great harbour; it was purely functional, catering for mercantile activities, shipping and pottery manufactured from the local clays. Poole is still an important port, though more now for leisure craft than merchant shipping.

BROWNSEA ISLAND CASTLE 1904 52801

Brownsea is the largest island in Poole Harbour and now belongs to the National Trust. In 1907, Robert Baden Powell held a camp for boys on the island, which laid the foundations for the Boy Scout movement, which he initiated not long afterwards.

POOLE, THE HARBOUR OFFICE 1904 52815
Close to the quays at Poole is the 18th-century Harbour Office, once the Old Town House, a club for ships captains. On the front of the building is an old sundial, and on the side a carving of Benjamin Skutt, who was Mayor of Poole in 1727.

POOLE, THE TOWN CELLARS 1887 19511
The cellars are situated in one of the oldest parts of town; we see it here on a busy day at the height of Poole's mercantile past. Poole had many independent breweries at this time; here we see one of their horse drawn drays on a delivery round.

POOLE

The Custom House 1904 52814

In 1747 a valuable cargo of tea was seized by the revenue
men and stored in the old Custom House at Poole. A
band of well-armed smugglers attacked the Custom
House in retaliation, seizing the tea and putting the
revenue men to flight. The tea mysteriously disappeared
inland on the back of a procession of packhorses.

POOLE, HIGH STREET 1900 46087

Poole developed along the banks of the finest natural harbour in England. It still maintains strong links with the sea, having become a mecca for yachtsmen. The prosperous town, built where the sea meets the wild heathlands of Dorset, is one of the largest along the south coast. Although spoiled by modern development, the tangle of streets around the old town is worth exploring and there is still much fine Georgian and Victorian architecture to be seen.

POOLE, HIGH STREET 1900 46088

Nowadays the greater part of Poole's population lives in the suburbs that have sprawled across the heathlands towards Bournemouth and Wimborne; but when this picture was taken, the residents mostly lived in the old town and around the quays, as they had for hundreds of years.

POOLE, HIGH STREET 1904 52808

Poole did not become a holiday resort in any conventional sense for many years, but remained important as a port and merchant centre. However, holidaymakers were discovering the delights of the town on day-trips, and some of the sandier areas of Poole Harbour were attracting tourists.

POOLE, LONGFLEET ROAD 1904 52811

Trams were an efficient form of transport, which lasted for a great many years in Poole. They harnessed the power of the newly-introduced electricity as the driving force, as we can see from the power lines above. Cyclists and pedestrians occasionally found the tramlines an extra hazard on Dorset's rough and ready roads.

POOLE
High Street 1908 61164
Much of the High Street is now pedestrianised as the town
comes to terms with modern day traffic pressures. Yet just
after midday on a busy Edwardian afternoon, the traffic is
a little less hectic: horses and carriages, pedal cycles and
pedestrians dominate the scene.

POOLE, THE PARK 1904 52802
With its fine views across the harbour, Poole Park became a popular gathering ground for tourists who wanted to walk, row boats or just sit in the sunshine.

POOLE, PARK LAKE 1908 61176
In 1890 the Prince of Wales opened Poole Park, once a forbidding swamp on the edge of the harbour, on land donated by Lord Wimborne. The park lake covers some 60 acres and serves for boating and as a sanctuary for tamer wildfowl.

POOLE, WATER SKIING AT ROCKLEY SANDS C1955 P72243
After the Second World War, holiday camps and caravan sites enjoyed a boom as rationing ended and people had more leisure time and money to spend.

POOLE, THE SUPERMARKET AT ROCKLEY SANDS C.1955 P72188
An early photograph of a supermarket. Newspapers commented at this time that supermarkets would never last as a shopping idea, because customers would resent the lack of personal service.

Bournemouth and Christchurch - New Dorset and Old Hampshire

STANDING on Bournemouth sea front on a summer's day, when it is most alive with the sights and sounds of thousands of tourists and the bustle of motor traffic, it is hard to grasp that less than two hundred years ago there was nothing to be seen except miles of wild heathland and no sound except the murmur of the sea. For Bournemouth is a town of recent origin. Had Mr Lewis Tregonwell decided to build his house somewhere else in 1810, there is a possibility that Bournemouth might never have existed. It took years, after Tregonwell's interference on what had been the lonely banks of the River Bourne, before the new town even approached its heyday as a family seaside resort.

Did anyone other than fishermen enjoy the seven glorious miles of sandy beaches for leisure, in the long centuries before Bournemouth was founded? We shall probably never know - but generations have discovered them since, and millions of people must retain affection for the town that provided them with their first seaside holiday.

Bournemouth could have been tailor-made as a touring centre for east Dorset and Hampshire. It is conveniently reached from everywhere, and a great deal of wild countryside still exists right up to the borders of this vast conurbation. Bournemouth, Poole and Christchurch together make up the largest urban mass on the Dorset coast.

Christchurch, originally called Twyneham, meaning the settlement between two rivers, offers picturesque scenery and admirable architecture. The Rivers Stour and Avon are long waterways, in contrast to most of the others along this coast, and flow across considerable stretches of the West Country. The added delights of this river scenery and the old-fashioned estuary at Mudeford complement the old priory town.

The church itself, once part of the historic priory which held such power and influence, and owned a great many manors throughout southern England, is arguably the finest medieval church in a county of grand churches. The nearby castle was built by the Normans to stamp their authority on what had been hitherto an important Saxon burgh. The church has survived where the castle has fallen, and the ruins of the latter now dominate the town less than the ecclesiastical buildings.

A stroll along the High Street reveals much interesting Georgian and Victorian architecture, not really spoiled by the modern shops and precinct.

Having come this distance along the Dorset coast, the traveller does not have to journey much further to pass out of the county altogether and into Hampshire, for the eastern end of Christchurch Bay is outside Dorset. A good place to reflect on the beauties of the coast is Hengistbury Head, which guards the harbour at Mudeford from the worst excesses of the tides and the Channel weather. Hengistbury was probably used as a lookout post by Roman and Saxon guards, yet the view looking back along the Dorset Coast is limited to Poole Bay and Durlston Head, beyond Swanage. An old Dorset seaman standing here once told a coastal walker who had rambled all the way from Lyme Regis, that this was how it should be; that the coast was too beautiful to behold all at once, and that in any case one should always look ahead and never back. The Dorset coast always stays with anyone who has ever visited it. Its lovely coves, long shorelines and sweeping downlands live in the memory forever.

BOURNEMOUTH, THE GARDENS 1904 52877
Bournemouth, once in Hampshire but now in Dorset, did not exist two hundred years ago. In 1810, Lewis Tregonwell built a house on lonely heathland close to the mouth of the River Bourne. During the years that followed other wealthy Hampshire gentlemen followed his example. It was to be the very end of the century before the town became popular as a holiday resort.

BOURNEMOUTH
The Square 1900 45218
Like so many seaside resorts of the 19th century,
Bournemouth attracted a wealthy clientele who built
numerous villas for semi-permanent and permanent
occupation. Here we see the carriages of the wealthy
assembled in the Square.

BOURNEMOUTH, THE SQUARE 1904 52874

The Square stands at the very heart of the town, astride the River Bourne. Since its early days as a resort, Bournemouth has striven to be the 'garden city by the sea', and its lovely flower displays are a famous attraction for visitors.

BOURNEMOUTH, THE SQUARE 1922 72695

By the 1920s Bournemouth had become a major south coast resort, rivalling Brighton and Torquay - and the traffic in the Square had increased accordingly, with private motor vehicles competing with the charabanc for parking spaces. The latter would take trippers to many beautiful localities nearby, such as Purbeck and the New Forest.

BOURNEMOUTH, THE SQUARE AND GARDENS 1925 78777

 By now the Square was beginning to show some degree of the traffic problems that were to blight the town in future years. As well as being a holiday resort, Bournemouth was gaining a reputation as a smart shopping town, and by the 1920s department stores were lining the main streets. The gardens around the square provided a pleasant refuge from the hurly-burly of 20th century life - and still do.

BOURNEMOUTH
Invalids' Walk 1900 45226
Bournemouth became a sanctuary for the rich and famous. Mary Shelley, creator of Frankenstein, lived here for many years and is buried in the town alongside the heart of her poet husband. Robert Louis Stevenson came to the coast here to benefit his health, and wrote 'Kidnapped' while in the town. Another famous visitor was King Edward VII, who discreetly entertained his mistress Lilly Langtry nearby.

BOURNEMOUTH, THE SQUARE 1933 85608

BOURNEMOUTH
The Square 1933
Today, the great conurbation that is Bournemouth has absorbed older settlements nearby and has linked up with the ancient towns of Christchurch and Poole. About a third of the population of Dorset now lives within the area.

◆

BOURNEMOUTH
Town Centre c1955
By the 1950s, Bournemouth was at the height of its popularity and one of the most prosperous towns in England, as this view of the town centre shows. At the height of the summer it became difficult to find an available bed in the resort's many hotels and guest houses. In the background here is the 200-foot high spire of St. Peter's church, which dominates the heart of Bournemouth.

BOURNEMOUTH, TOWN CENTRE c1955 B163109

BOURNEMOUTH, THE HERBERT HOME, WESTBOURNE 1892 31371

Westbourne, on the west side of Bournemouth, retains a village atmosphere even today, with spacious houses and hotels situated around an attractive woodland chine leading down to the sea. It has some of the best clifftop views in the area, overlooking the broad waters of Poole Bay.

BOURNEMOUTH, EAST CLIFF FROM THE WEST 1897 40556

Because of the unstable nature of the cliffs above Bournemouth's beaches, many of the buildings were built at a distance from the cliff edge. Here we are looking at East Cliff towards Boscombe and Southbourne from the rising gradient of West Cliff.

BOURNEMOUTH
East Cliff 1897 40562

This view, with well-clad visitors strolling along the beach and sailing boats drawn up on the shore, shows a south coast beach before development and formalisation changed its character. Even so long ago, the trappings of a modern seaside resort were starting to appear.

BOURNEMOUTH, WEST CLIFF FROM THE EAST 1897 40558

Early visitors preferred to stay in the hotels and villas in this area, within easy walking distance of the sea. The parasols were used to provide shade from the bright sun.

BOURNEMOUTH, PIER ENTRANCE 1900 45213

Bournemouth Pier stands above the original mouth of the River Bourne. Its construction marked the town's commitment to its role as a resort. The mildness of the climate first attracted visitors to the town, and it rapidly acquired a reputation as a place beneficial to consumptives.

BOURNEMOUTH, THE PIER 1925 78768

A busier view of Bournemouth Pier attracting strollers and sightseers. The Pier has undergone several transformations since it was first built, but retains its popularity.

BOURNEMOUTH, THE PIER 1908 61180

Only a century after its foundation, the town was already dominating the skyline and its beaches were among the most crowded on the south coast. Thomas Hardy described the town as 'Sandbourne' in his novel 'The Hand of Ethelberta', and immortalised it in 'Tess of the D'Urbervilles' as 'the city of detached mansions'.

BOURNEMOUTH, THE SWANAGE BOAT 1908 61183
Given that this part of the coast had a small number of harbours, the coastal pleasure boats were moored alongside Bournemouth's Pier. Here we see the Swanage boat about to set sail on a calm day.

BOURNEMOUTH, THE BEACH 1922 72687
It would be interesting to know just what the Frith photographer made of the competition from the 'Happy Holiday Snaps' kiosk that is attracting so much custom at the edge of the sands!

BOSCOMBE
The Pier 1908
Boscombe developed to the east of Bournemouth in mid-Victorian times, attracting the wealthy and fashionable including Sir Percy Florence Shelley, the son of the poet. Mineral springs added to Boscombe's attraction for those seeking an improvement to health, though it never became the spa that it aspired to be.

◆

BOSCOMBE
From the Pier 1918
Like Bournemouth's Pier, the structure at Boscombe was severely damaged in the Second World War, but both have been sympathetically restored. A third pier at Southbourne did not survive.

BOSCOMBE, THE PIER 1908 61191

BOSCOMBE, FROM THE PIER 1918 68076

BOSCOMBE, FROM THE PIER 1903 49158

Looking the other way, we see paddlers and bathing machines. As at Bournemouth, the houses stand back from the unstable cliffs, though steep paths zigzag down them to provide access to the beaches.

BOSCOMBE, FISHERMEN'S WALK 1913 66138

Boscombe was built across a wooded chine (a wide ravine) that led down to the sea; these features are common along this coast. Since this photograph was taken, many of the quieter strolls have been formalised into pretty flower-filled gardens, where tourists and locals alike can sit and contemplate on pleasant days.

BOSCOMBE, THE BATHING BEACH 1925 78783

By the 1920s, bathing costumes had become more practical than those shown in the previous illustrations, and the bathing machines had become redundant in favour of smaller kiosks and tents. Beach huts, which could be rented on a weekly basis, have become a feature of the seaside scene.

BOSCOMBE, CHRISTCHURCH ROAD 1892 31381

Christchurch Road, seen here as it enters Boscombe, must be one of the longest streets in England, as it runs the full distance between Bournemouth and Christchurch. Though quiet in the year of the photograph, it became notorious for traffic jams in the next century.

BOSCOMBE, THE ARCADE 1892 31380

The Arcade became one of the most fashionable shopping streets in the area. The gothic architecture remained an enthusiasm for builders and architects throughout the late Victorian period.

SOUTHBOURNE, FROM THE PIER 1908 61203

Southbourne has an unfortunate place in aviation history as the scene of the air crash that killed the pioneer pilot Mr Rolls, of Rolls Royce fame, in 1910. Rolls was the first person to die in a British air accident. The downlands above the cliffs were popular with early aviators until Southbourne became too built up.

SOUTHBOURNE, THE CLIFF RAILWAY c1955 S153115
The cliff railway provided an easy way to descend to the seven miles of golden beaches that can be enjoyed by the holidaymaker in Bournemouth.

SOUTHBOURNE, FISHERMAN'S WALK 1922 72714

SOUTHBOURNE
Fisherman's Walk 1922
Some local people tried to continue making a living in the old trades. Small fishing boats would be launched off the beaches for many years after the first tourists arrived; fishermen would also offer boat trips to visitors.

CHRISTCHURCH
Wick Ferry Holiday Camp c1955
The holiday camp phenomenon had been developed by Billy Butlin before the Second World War. By the 1950s, the popularity of a cheap and cheerful holiday camp atmosphere brought thousands of visitors to camps like Wick Ferry each year.

CHRISTCHURCH, WICK FERRY HOLIDAY CAMP c1955 C99156

CHRISTCHURCH, WICK FERRY HOLIDAY CAMP c1955 C99150
Much of the entertainment at Wick Ferry was organised by camp staff, who would arrange competitions and participation shows involving the campers. There was a strong element of compulsion in these events, and woe betide the campers who refused to throw themselves into the spirit of the occasion!

CHRISTCHURCH, WICK FERRY HOLIDAY CAMP c1955 C99166
The model steam train was a popular attraction, as it took campers along the edge of the Holiday Park.

HIGHCLIFFE, THE CASTLE 1900 45059

HIGHCLIFFE
The Castle 1900
Highcliffe Castle, near Christchurch, once one of the grandest stately homes in Hampshire, has been undergoing major restoration in recent years to bring it back to its former glory. The grade 1 listed building was built by Lord Stuart de Rothesay in the Romantic style between 1830 and 1835, employing the famous London architect William Donthorpe.

◆

MUDEFORD
The Promenade c1955
Looking out onto Christchurch Bay, Mudeford remains the centre of the fishing industry in the area, though not usually on such stormy days as this one. Despite some hideous modern development, Mudeford retains its attraction for visitors who come to enjoy the sea and watch fishermen at work.

MUDEFORD, THE PROMENADE c1955 M106017

MUDEFORD, THE SAND HILLS 1934 86276

Sheltered from the worst of the Channel gales by Hengistbury Head, Christchurch Harbour empties into the sea between the quays and Mudeford sandbank. Salmon are netted and crabs caught here by local fishermen, and dinghies sailed by locals and holidaymakers alike.

CHRISTCHURCH, THE RIVER 1918 68052

Christchurch (or Christchurch Twyneham, to give the town its old name) is one of the oldest settlements on the south coast, probably being in existence even before the Romans settled in the shelter of Hengistbury Head sometime after 43 AD. It owes its continued existence to the patronage of the Saxon kings of Wessex and its adoption by the later Normans.

CHRISTCHURCH, PRIORY CHURCH FROM THE CASTLE 1906 55905

The Saxon church was demolished by the Normans in 1095 and the present building, the longest parish church in England, built in its place. Legend says that the church was originally destined for nearby St Catherine's Hill, but the building materials kept being mysteriously moved to the present site. A strange carpenter suddenly appeared to help raise the rafters with such perfection that the new place of worship was named Christchurch in his honour.

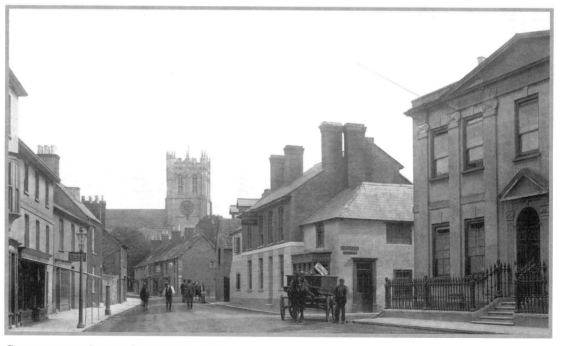

CHRISTCHURCH, CHURCH STREET 1900 45053

This view shows a working community - the town still thrives today. Until around 1900, fishing was still a major industry in Christchurch, though its port never really developed beyond the present simple harbour.

CHRISTCHURCH, HIGH STREET 1900 45043

The street has much fine Georgian and Victorian architecture. Leading up to the castle and priory, the High Street has always been the focus of the town. It is interesting to remember that trade prospered in this historic street for centuries before a single house stood in neighbouring Bournemouth.

CHRISTCHURCH BLACKWATER FERRY 1900 45048

Christchurch stands on two rivers, the Stour and the Avon, and gets its old name of Twyneham from the Anglo Saxon, meaning 'the town between the rivers'. Here the ferryman at Blackwater pulls the ferry across the water using a rope as propulsion.

Index

Frith Book Co 1999 Titles

From 2000 we aim at publishing 100 new books each year. For latest catalogue please contact Frith Book Co

Barnstaple	1-85937-084-5	£12.99	Oct 99
Blackpool	1-85937-049-7	£12.99	Sep 99
Bognor Regis	1-85937-055-1	£12.99	Sep 99
Bristol	1-85937-050-0	£12.99	Sep 99
Cambridge	1-85937-092-6	£12.99	Oct 99
Cambridgeshire	1-85937-086-1	£14.99	Nov 99
Cheshire	1-85937-045-4	£14.99	Sep 99
Chester	1-85937-090-X	£12.99	Nov 99
Chesterfield	1-85937-071-3	£12.99	Sep 99
Chichester	1-85937-089-6	£12.99	Nov 99
Cornwall	1-85937-054-3	£14.99	Sep 99
Cotswolds	1-85937-099-3	£14.99	Nov 99

Maidstone	1-85937-056-X	£12.99	Sep 99
Northumberland & Tyne and Wear	1-85937-072-1	£14.99	Sep 99
North Yorkshire	1-85937-048-9	£14.99	Sep 99
Nottingham	1-85937-060-8	£12.99	Sep 99
Oxfordshire	1-85937-076-4	£14.99	Oct 99
Penzance	1-85937-069-1	£12.99	Sep 99
Reading	1-85937-087-X	£12.99	Nov 99
St Ives	1-85937-068-3	£12.99	Sep 99
Salisbury	1-85937-091-8	£12.99	Nov 99
Scarborough	1-85937-104-3	£12.99	Sep 99
Scottish Castles	1-85937-077-2	£14.99	Oct 99
Sevenoaks and Tonbridge	1-85937-057-8	£12.99	Sep 99
Sheffield and S Yorkshire	1-85937-070-5	£12.99	Sep 99
Shropshire	1-85937-083-7	£14.99	Nov 99
Southampton	1-85937-088-8	£12.99	Nov 99
Staffordshire	1-85937-047-0	£14.99	Sep 99
Stratford upon Avon	1-85937-098-5	£12.99	Nov 99
Suffolk	1-85937-074-8	£14.99	Oct 99
Surrey	1-85937-081-0	£14.99	Oct 99
Torbay	1-85937-063-2	£12.99	Sep 99
Wiltshire	1-85937-053-5	£14.99	Sep 99

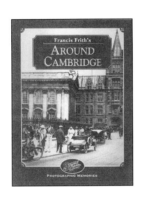

Derby	1-85937-046-2	£12.99	Sep 99
Devon	1-85937-052-7	£14.99	Sep 99
Dorset	1-85937-075-6	£14.99	Oct 99
Dorset Coast	1-85937-062-4	£14.99	Sep 99
Dublin	1-85937-058-6	£12.99	Sep 99
East Anglia	1-85937-059-4	£14.99	Sep 99
Eastbourne	1-85937-061-6	£12.99	Sep 99
English Castles	1-85937-078-0	£14.99	Oct 99
Essex	1-85937-082-9	£14.99	Nov 99
Falmouth	1-85937-066-7	£12.99	Sep 99
Hampshire	1-85937-064-0	£14.99	Sep 99
Hertfordshire	1-85937-079-9	£14.99	Nov 99
Isle of Man	1-85937-065-9	£14.99	Sep 99
Liverpool	1-85937-051-9	£12.99	Sep 99

British Life A Century Ago
246 x 189mm
144pp, hardback.
Black and white
Lavishly illustrated with photos from the turn of the century, and with extensive commentary. It offers a unique insight into the social history and heritage of bygone Britain.

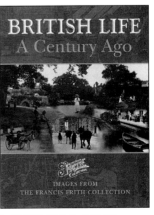

1-85937-103-5 £17.99 ....

Available from your local bookshop or from the publisher

FRITH PRODUCTS & SERVICES

Francis Frith would doubtless be pleased to know that the pioneering publishing venture he started in 1860 still continues today. More than a hundred and thirty years later, The Francis Frith Collection continues in the same innovative tradition and is now one of the foremost publishers of vintage photographs in the world. Some of the current activities include:

Interior Decoration

Today Frith's photographs can be seen framed and as giant wall murals in thousands of pubs, restaurants, hotels, banks, retail stores and other public buildings throughout the country. In every case they enhance the unique local atmosphere of the places they depict and provide reminders of gentler days in an increasingly busy and frenetic world.

Product Promotions

Frith products have been used by many major companies to promote the sales of their own products or to reinforce their own history and heritage. Brands include Hovis bread, Courage beers, Scots Porage Oats, Colman's mustard, Cadbury's foods, Mellow Birds coffee, Dunhill pipe tobacco, Guinness, and Bulmer's Cider.

Genealogy and Family History

As the interest in family history and roots grows world-wide, more and more people are turning to Frith's photographs of Great Britain for images of the towns, villages and streets where their ancestors lived; and, of course, photographs of the churches and chapels where their ancestors were christened, married and buried are an essential part of every genealogy tree and family album.

A series of easy-to-use CD Roms is planned for publication, and an increasing number of Frith photographs will be able to be viewed on specialist genealogy sites. A growing range of Frith books will be available on CD.

The Internet

Already thousands of Frith photographs can be viewed and purchased on the internet. By the end of the year 2000 some 60,000 Frith photographs will be available on the internet. The number of sites is constantly expanding, each focussing on different products and services from the Collection.

Some of the sites are listed below.

www.townpages.co.uk
www.familystorehouse.com
www.britannia.com
www.icollector.com
www.barclaysquare.co.uk
www.cornwall-online.co.uk

For background information on the Collection look at the two following sites:

www.francisfrith.com
www.francisfrith.co.uk

Frith Products

All Frith photographs are available Framed or just as Mounted Prints, and can be ordered from the address below. From time to time other products - Address Books, Calendars, Table Mats, Postcards etc - are available.

The Frith Collectors' Guild

In response to the many customers who enjoy collecting Frith photographs we have created the Frith Collectors' Guild. Members are entitled to a range of benefits, including a regular magazine, special discounts and special limited edition products.

For further information: if you would like further information on any of the above aspects of the Frith business please contact us at the address below:

The Francis Frith Collection, Frith's Barn, Teffont, Salisbury, Wiltshire England SP3 5QP.

Tel: +44 (0) 1722 716 376 Fax: +44 (0) 1722 716 881   Email: frithbook.co.uk

To receive your FREE Mounted Print

Cut out this Voucher and return it with your remittance for £1.50 to cover postage and handling. Choose any photograph included in this book. Your SEPIA print will be A4 in size, and mounted in a cream mount with burgundy rule lines, overall size 14 x 11 inches.

Order additional Mounted Prints at HALF PRICE (only £7.49 each*)

If there are further pictures you would like to order, possibly as gifts for friends and family, acquire them at half price (no additional postage and handling required).

Have your Mounted Prints framed*

For an additional £14.95 per print you can have your chosen Mounted Print framed in an elegant polished wood and gilt moulding, overall size 16 x 13 inches (no additional postage and handling required).

---

* IMPORTANT!
These special prices are only available if ordered using the original voucher on this page (no copies permitted) and at the same time as your free Mounted Print, for delivery to the same address

---

Voucher for FREE and Reduced Price Frith Prints

Picture no.	Page number	Qty	Mounted @ £7.49	Framed + £14.95	Total Cost
		1	**Free of charge***	£	£
			£	£	£
			£	£	£
			£	£	£
			£	£	£
			£	£	£
			* Post & handling		£1.50
			Total Order Cost		£

Title: DORSET COAST
062-4

Please do not photocopy this voucher. Only the original is valid, so please cut it out and return it to us.

I enclose a cheque / postal order for £ . . . .
made payable to 'The Francis Frith Collection'
OR please debit my Mastercard / Visa / Switch / Amex card

Number . . . .

Expires . . . .   Signature . . . .

Name Mr/Mrs/Ms . . . .

Address . . . .

. . . .

. . . .

. . . .

. . . . Postcode . . . .

Daytime Tel No . . . .   Valid to 31/12/01

Frith Collectors' Guild

From time to time we publish a magazine of news and stories about Frith photographs and further special offers of Frith products. If you would like 12 months FREE membership, please return this form and we will send you a New Member Pack.

Send completed forms to:
The Francis Frith Collection, Frith's Barn, Teffont, Salisbury, Wiltshire SP3 5QP

The Francis Frith Collectors' Guild

I would like to receive the New Members Pack offering 12 months FREE membership.

062-4

Name Mr/Mrs/Ms . . . .

Address . . . .

. . . .

. . . .

. . . . Postcode . . . .